The Poetic Courier

Genetta Brown Turner

authorHOUSE®

AuthorHouse™
1663 Liberty Drive
Bloomington, IN 47403
www.authorhouse.com
Phone: 1-800-839-8640

Published by AuthorHouse   01/24/2015

ISBN: 978-1-4969-5624-8 (sc)
ISBN: 978-1-4969-5625-5 (e)

KJV

*Scripture quotations marked KJV are from the Holy Bible, King James Version
(Authorized Version). First published in 1611. Quoted from the KJV Classic
Reference Bible, Copyright © 1983 by The Zondervan Corporation.*

Contents

THE POETIC COURIER I

THE POETIC COURIER II

THE POETIC COURIER III

THE POETIC COURIER I

These poems are inspired by my sister Veronica, who has written the Poetic Messenger Part 1 and 2. Rest in Peace Baby Girl!

Family and Friends have also inspired some of the poems in the Poetic Courier as well, I thank you all for that inspiration.

Thanks to Lewis Turner Jr., Isaac Turner and Vincent Turner. I could not have done this without all of you.

The Poetic
Courier

Illustration
JB...

This is the day the lord has made

This is the day that the lord has made, I will rejoice and be glad in it

Even though my sunny day turned to dark clouds of gray,

I will trust in the lord, Jesus because he is truth and life,

He'll always make a way

I felt my sister's spirit going Heaven bound

To my dismay she's no longer around

Then suddenly, sunlight came from that dark, depressing cloud

Now my sister's heartbeat can be heard in Heaven, Strong and Loud.

From dust she came, From this Earth, From Light

She is given life in Heaven, a Rebirth

This is the day that the lord has made, I will rejoice and be glad in it.

Diamond in the rough

I met you in front of church, so handsome and so kind

Your glimmer shined so brightly, I had to make you mine.

We both went to the alter and got saved.

But Satan tried to fool us,

By making us doubt our love,

And trying to make us his slave.

Two hearts that became one as we wed

We sometimes sacrificed our salvation

For which Jesus' Blood was shed

Though we were not perfect,

And made mistakes alone the way,

Our love for each other shined brighter every day.

Now you're in Heaven, and it's really tough

Because you're still a diamond

My Diamond in the Rough

All my sisters go to Heaven

All my sisters go to Heaven,

First there were nine girls, now there are eight.

Some people say death is a part of life and that it is everyone's fate,

All my sisters go to Heaven,

There used to be eight girls, now there are seven

Are the roads paved with gold in Heaven?

All my sisters go to Heaven,

May the circle be unbroken bye and bye.

All my sisters go to Heaven, where we meet each other in the sky

There's a better home waiting in the sky, where the Lord waits for us;

All my sister's go to Heaven!

Time stood still when you went away

Time stood still when you went away!

LeBron did what? Kim did what? Kanye what's up?

Plane crash where? Are you still there?

Today is old news because it just seems to fade away!

The news is that you are no longer around and that's why I'm feeling so down today!

I miss us talking on the phone, when you were bed ridden and all alone,

To see you smile one more day and pray to God that you're ok.

Time moved fast and passed us by, now I'm sad and thinking of the time

We won't share on this Earth makes me cry.

Looking in your eyes knowing your end was near,

Trying to give us both strength and conquer our fears;

The fear of leaving too soon.

Time was not very kind in June,

Weeks past and I prayed every day,

When that time stood still and you went away!

Cancer

A tricky dastardly disease has no mercy on its victims,

Leaving them unable to walk or talk or even move.

Some people even lose their ability to breath, causing a slow painful death.

Leaving families financially burdened and tricky treatments that are very hard to prove.

God's mercy has the last say,

So one day this disease will fade away,

Hopefully this will come soon so this disease will be in the past,

And then life will be the cure for the future

Life is the cure!

The last straw

Nobody's perfect, everyone has flaws that make them come up short in their lives,

But this is the last straw!

I called you on the phone, and you didn't pick up.

Are you ok?

Of course you are.

You were just drinking, thinking, or sinking into a stupor to forget all your troubles,

Also including myself.

That's how you handle life or go through life,

Like a game and you're winning all the time, because you think it's all about you

But it's not!

Life is never selfish or conceited, it's about love and how you love.

(And you haven't even been doing that lately.)

I guess your heart is frozen and it needs to thaw

Everyone has flaws, this is my last straw.

A letter to my sister

A letter to my sister

You will always be in my heart!

One of the last conversations I had with you,

Was when you said you wanted to go sky diving and I said it wouldn't be safe thing to do,

We both started laughing.

Being the adventurous spirit that you are, I know that you are sky diving in Heaven,

And the clouds have picked up your spirit,

And now you are free.

Love making

Kissing and hugging

Caressing and loving

Squeezing and teasing

Poking and stroking

Endless serenity

Up and down, all around

This is love making

A feeling of euphoria

Never faking an orgasm

Coming down slowly

And doing it all over again

This is love making

Ballad of the backslider

Once a Christian, always a Christian, that's what church folk say.

But when the enemy infiltrate, which is Satan, you joy is swept away.

He will tell you it's ok what the World does,

Then talk about and mock you, even call you a fool!

The battle starts when the candle is lit,

Then you go around saying you're saved

When your really a hypocrite.

But you see what was done in darkness will soon come to light,

Then everyone finds out you really weren't right with Christ in your life..

Being a pretender is a terrible thing to be,

Especially when one knows all the gifts Christ can offer you.

So if you lose contact with God's grace,

Just ask for guidance and seek the savior's face.

Then repent and let Christ back into your heart,

Because salvation is a gift from God and it will never depart.

Daddy! Father God can you hear me?

It's been a long time since my earthly father passed away.

Now two of his children are in Heaven with him, I hope you all are ok.

They are wrapped in our heavenly father God arms and the tears are rolling down his face.

But these are tears of joy because no one can take our heavenly father's place.

We are all his children and he has taken care of us all, he will even catch us when we fall.

Three of your children are with you now, and I am missing all of you.

Someday we will see one another in Heaven, but now I am feeling blue.

Because I am still on this Earth, there is so much fear, but when we all get to Heaven,

That's when we all will cheer!

Because Heaven is a good place to be.

Where people live forever and are happy and free.

Daddy! Father God in Heaven can you hear me?

A peaceful evening

Sometimes when I am in my home and the air conditioner is on, it feels so cold and freezing.

Then I go outside in the evening and the wind is blowing on my face, it is breezing, so relaxing, and easy.

It's hard to describe what I'm feeling, a calm freeing of my spirit, and my sol at ease.

Dancing and prancing to its own tune are the trees.

The weather seems so perfect, peaceful, and still.

Yet my soul is at ease and I am trying to figure out how I feel.

Seeing the beauty of the sky and the grass blowing, its movement is so synchronized,

And I think that the Earth is happy and is God and Heavens.

A ball of confusion

When I'm asking all the time a ball of confusion runs through my mind

What is a ball of confusion you say? It's just living from day to day.

And as I wonder what is this life all about,

A feeling on confusion comes over me and I start to doubt, what this world is all about.

Why are there so many wars and rumors of war and if there's war, what are we fighting for?

Is this just a delusion that will disappear with time, or will this ball of confusion remain in my mind?

They say that it's just one of life's phases, and that confusion can make a person dazed.

Do you understand where I'm coming from? Or am I a victim of my own ball of confusion.

Let us pray

Let us pray when things are not going our way and we are living from paycheck to paycheck day by day.

Let us pray when our kids are hungry and there is no food around and there is no money to be found.

Let us pray when young men rob banks and run, and the police keep killing our youth with guns.

Let us pray when we send our sons and daughters to fight a war, when it's their life we should secure.

Let us pray for peace when there is no peace around, and war is all we've found.

Let us pray for life and safety and love every day. Let us pray.

The poetic messenger

The rose on your book makes me think of love, a love that is very rare and comes from above.

The poetic messages you wrote come from your heart and those kinds of messages will never depart.

God gave special people gifts to put their feelings into words, things we experience in our life is so real.

Poetry is a way to write how a person feels.

Simplicity comes to mind when I read them, I understand them,

They are inspired by you and the words in these poems are tributes to you.

Your rose for life on this Earth has withered and faded away.

But then your spirit bloomed out from that rose, and those words are here to stay.

Baby daddies

A baby daddy is like a sperm donor. He'll never marry because he has no honor.

Maybe because it was one those one night stands, and the next day he won't even hold your hands.

He's not there for his baby girl, while you take the heat and just like the typical guy he is a dead beat.

Not paying child support because he thinks money is going to fall out of the sky.

Jesus loves the little children so why should I, he says.

Action speaks louder than words and there is no interaction, so your words are never heard.

You just go on letting grandma and grandpa be father and mother.

While your responsibility gets further and further, "out of sight" out of mind.

You are just a sperm donor wasting my time.

Marriage

God gift that two people share life together as one.

The children spring up from that reunion, so that's half the fun.

Having a soul mate that will always stick around, these are secrets of good marriage.

Just open the lock with the key and the answer will be found.

It comes when you and your mate are sleeping in the same bed, giving oneself to one another.

Like when Jesus blood was shed, two people becoming one spiritual body creating life.

These are just some of the things you feel, when you become husband and wife.

Message in a bottle

I am a messenger in a bottle, won't you open me?

This month for me has been pretty rough.

If I had a message, then it would say,

That I have been missing you every day.

A message of hope that there will be brighter days.

So let the sun shine its rays! I need a message of hope and joy.

So sing the halleluiah choir, I need a message of peace.

So cut that calf and break bread and feast.

A message of love that comes from above,

A message of praise so we can raise the roof,

And feel God's spirit of truth.

The truth that will set us free, because we were blind,

But know we see that Jesus is the light of the world.

I found that message in the bottle and it's with me all the time,

No longer in that bottle, now in my mind.

That message of love, peace and joy never will depart.

That bottle has now been replaced and resides in my heart.

Shine a light at the end of the tunnel

When all hope is lost and your faith is gone.

Shine a light at the end of the tunnel.

When they said you'd never amount to anything and they closed the door,

You said here I am, signed, sealed, delivered, I'm yours.

Shine a light at the end of the tunnel.

When everyone left you and your friends could not be found, I'll be around.

Shine a light at the end of the tunnel.

When they shot you just for hanging around that bag of skittles fell to the ground.

Shine a light at the end of the tunnel.

When you were sick and did not have health insurance and the government was not around.

Now there is support and we are health care bound.

Shine a light at the end of the tunnel.

When they tried to break you, make you, feel like your world was tumbling down

You had faith and stood your ground.

Shine a light at the end of the tunnel.

We won't go back; we'll keep going until we see the light shining at the end of the tunnel.

Celebrations

It is time to celebrate,

For these are very special dates

Like a time when we are born, so pluck the harp and blow the horn;

For life has just begun.

Celebrations come in many forms,

Weddings are special days, when two people give themselves to one another, in a civil way.

Holidays are special too.

Thanksgiving and Christmas just to name a few.

Graduations are so much fun,

When all our academic work is done.

It's a great feeling and so appealing to celebrate life's ups and downs.

To celebrate life's accomplishments, as we march in our cap and gowns.

There are other ways we celebrate with soldiers in their stations,

Like the 4th of July, we celebrate the independence of our nation.

Celebrations are just one way we can show our love ones that we appreciate them,

In special ways and special days so that their lives are remembered and cherished forever.

Miscommunication

My niece sent me a text message which said my mother was dying.

As I was reading this text I was crying.

Has life gotten so impersonal that a text is the best you can do

To get through to your family to send bad news.

What about picking up a phone and talking, that's how it used to be done.

Will there be a text from God when Jesus comes.

Why can't we look each other straight in the eyes?

While life passes us by.

Can you text a hug or a kiss.

Is there something that I missed?

How about a laugh or a smile.

Or would that come under E- file.

Done text me, respect me.

I'm a human, not a computer, write me, call me, don't text me.

Panic Attack!

When my husband died, everyone left, and then I cried,

Then later on that evening my spirit was broken, now I'm grieving.

It's a feeling you wouldn't wish on your worst enemy.

Walking around in a daze, a friend of mine said, "You'll be alright, it's just a phase."

But it wasn't just a phase, the feelings were real, and who is he to tell me how I feel.

It's like your swimming in a pool, but there's no water around, then you reach the surface

And there's no air to be found.

So you think to yourself, "Is there something I'm lacking?"

These are the first signs of a panic attack!

Thinking of good times you spent when that loved one was around.

Now that the loved one is in the ground.

How can this be! I just saw him or her the other day, now in this casket he laid.

Such a cruel and foul joke that's hard for anyone to cope.

And memories upon memories, they are stacked.

Just makes me anxious and cause another panic attack!

Showers and baths

When I take a shower or bathe, it's relaxing.

It takes the dirt and pain from stressing.

Worrying about things that I can't change.

I just pray to God and he will ease the pain.

People are all alone, losing their homes

Feeling the pressure of life day to day.

Soaking away their troubles and cares

Makes life a little easier to bare.

Sometimes when I go outside and look at all the flowers.

I thank the Lord up above that I can take a shower.

So many people need a place to lay their head

And their children don't even have a bed.

I am blessed because I have a home, in Heaven and on Earth.

Pain

Pain is when you heart aches and your body shakes.

We feel the pain when we go through things.

Things that are unpleasant and tragic are the worst kind.

Ii's like a bullet that pierces through your soul when your favorite team loses the super bowl.

When we go through life, we will have pain,

Just like the sun, there will be rain.

The way we choose to live through challenges is what makes us able to sustain.

Because as long as we're on God's green Earth, there will be pain.

Life

Life is a gift you and me

It set our hearts and souls so free,

Life is love, living and praying, waiting for love while delaying.

Life is when a baby cries,

And life is when that person dies.

Suffering

Come to me my suffering little child.

And I'm the one who can set you free.

Who the son of man set free is free indeed.

This is how God meant for it to be

Weeping will last for a short time,

But joy will come in the morning light.

Suffering is not your battle to fight.

Just give me all your troubles and cares.

And I will always be there to hold your hand and let you understand,

That I'm your number one fan.

And once you get to Heaven,

You will never suffer again.

Babysitting my mother

When I was young my mother was there,

She took us to church and really did care.

There was so many of us around,

Eight girls and two boys to be exact.

Daddy was working all the time and hardly was around.

But I had my brothers and sisters so that made up a lot of ground.

As mother grew older daddy passed away.

She did her best to raise the rest of us.

Not only did she raise her babies, she also raised their babies.

But as my mother grew older,

She grew kind of colder, not wanting anyone near,

Because she had a fear that her life was all about her children, never about her.

Then she wanted to be alone in her big beautiful home,

And pushed us away, so no one wanted to stay.

Now she's frail and she's the one that needed us to help her and take care of her.

So we feed her, change her, and spend time with her a bit.

Because she was always there for us, now we babysit.

It's ok to feel

It's ok to feel

When the pain is too hard to bare and no one seems to care,

It's ok to feel.

An emotion so simple, yet hard to describe.

Even professionals and scholars have tried

To feel the water when it rains down from the sky

And the Earth and creatures need to feel the rain to survive.

It's ok to happy or sad.

And when you are sick, you feel pretty bad!

It's ok to feel like this world owes you something,

When nobody gives anything.

In this world we feel what we want to feel,

Whether it's fake or real

It's ok to feel.

Lord, what do I need to do?

When I am hurt, I go to church,

And pray that I wake up another day and that you will stay in my heart and never depart.

Because I don't have to be alone on my own.

I want to be free and seek the Glory of your Holy presence

And fill me with your Holy Spirit,

So I can see that with you is where I want to be.

What do I need to do?

Have faith and believe that he will be there through good times and bad.

Happy and sad.

Through it all, what I need to do is to believe.

We all are God's children

Jesus loves the little children,

All kinds, yellow, black, white, red, it doesn't matter, because his blood was shed for all.

We are all God's children because he is worthy.

My god is an awesome God, his grace, and mercy endures forever.

He is the beginning and the end.

Glory be to our God.

The poetic courier

After my sister died, I tried to write poems to ease the pain.

As I wrote these poems, I felt whole again, it was a way to ease my mind.

Knowing that my sister was saved and gave her life to Christ before she died,

It made it easier to cope with, because I know she's in a better place.

These poems were written with joy and a whole lot of pain,

But I know I will see her once again.

Losing loved ones is a lot of grief

But if we stick to our beliefs we can go through all trials and tribulations.

These poems are a tribute to life's beginning and ending.

And life's many celebrations.

THE POETIC COURIER II

Welcome to Heaven

Genetta Brown Turner

Special Thanks to Isaac, Vincent and Lewis Turner

Lord, you are all we need!

In leaving this earth my sister Veronica is given a rebirth and a realm in heaven.

Because she loved and gave her life and trust to the lord,

She now resides in a kingdom in heaven.

Her heart and her spirit will always be a part of mine,

The love that we shared on this earth is heavenly divine.

A dedicated servant, she faced death with dignity.

And because of Jesus Christ she resides in heaven, because she is now free.

Lord, you are all we need!

A time for grieving

Every life has a purpose on this earth, every soul has a reason.

God made the sun and the earth and the summer, winter and all seasons

But when that life comes to an end, that's the time for grieving

A time to reflect on what impact that person has had on your life

And what they meant to you.

The special times you shared and cared for each other, too.

It's also a time to say goodbye to those who hold specials places in our hearts.

Grieving is the process of healing and a brand new start.

It can hurt and make you cry

When we say our farewells and final goodbyes.

But when that life comes to an end that's the time for grieving.

One thing is reassuring that through the pain we will see each other again

And our time for grieving will end and we will rejoice.

You have earned your wings

Welcome to heaven! Where you were meant to be. Because you trusted in God

Now you are free!

You have visited Earth and stay on land,

And ask God for answers when we took your hands.

Now, you're in heaven, and you have earned your wings.

You put your trust in God and that was freeing, you are now an angel

No longer a human being, because you had faith and believed you have earned you're wings.

In that sweet by and by you can now fly, and now in heavens doors you see.

You have earned your wings.

By seeing the lord's knowledge now you understand,

That with his help you have left this Earthly land.

When the gate opened you walked right in, and was forgiven of your sins,

This is where your life truly begins. And as the trumpet sound and the angels sing.

You have earned your wings.

As you walk through heaven you are smiling, praying, singing, and dancing.

The mansion you live in is so beautiful and fancy.

You have earned your wings.

Let the lord be magnified and his mercy endure, forever.

When the sun comes out

When the sun come out! We will scream and shout to the Lord.

When we pray and shout the spirit of the Lord will shine through!

So let us pray and shout until the sun comes out and all our work is done.

So let us pray and shout until the sun comes out, and the spirit of the Lord shine through!

Then wind will blow, and I truly know, that the spirit of the Lord shines through!

When the sun comes out, and the sky is blue, we'll sing and praise God's name.

But when the rain comes down, we will see the light of the sun of man.

Because when we praise God's name the sun will always shine,

And he will be in our hearts all the time.

When the sun comes out, there will be brighter days,

When my time on Earth ends,

And the realm of Heaven doors will shine its holy rays;

There in his presence I'll spend the rest of my days.

Praise God and his magnificent glory!

When the sun comes out, I won't be afraid,

Because Jesus will be my comforter in all my glory days.

He will shine his light, and his spirit and mercy will shined through.

When the sun comes out we will pray and shout

To the son of man, and he will take us by the hand and let us understand,

That his mercy and his glory, will tell the whole story,

Of how much he loves his children.

Welcome home my child, you have been set free!

When the sun comes out, I will pray and shout that the spirit of the Lord Shined through.

Agape love

What is Agape love you say?

It's just an eternal love that will never go away!

An everlasting love that comes from above,

It's when God sent his son Jesus to die for our sins,

And it is a love that will never end.

An unconditional love that will give us a new start, a love that comes from above,

And now live in our hearts.

And it's because of this, our precious Savior lives on God's throne we shall ask him for strength to carry on.

It is when the Lord has given us a brand new start and his grace and mercy,

Has given us a brand new heart, and he has forgiven us of all sin.

It's when we ask God to wipe our weeping eyes, and forgive our sins, because we gave our hearts and soul to him.

So when we see the gates of Heaven open we shall live again!

Now, Agape loves live within.

God gave his all when he gave his son Jesus, so when all our trials are over

We shall see our heavenly father's face.

We will be blessed by his holiness and grace, because we believed and received

The Lord, Jesus as our savior,

Agape love will give us favor. It is his grace and mercy that has forgiven us of all

Sins, and now AGAPE love lives within, now the Lord has given us and a new start,

With a brand new heart. And his Holy Spirit will live in our hearts forever.

What does the Lord require us to do?

The Lord needs our hearts so he can live within

With his spirit we can win.

Accept the Lord, Jesus as our savior

His sweet spirit is colorless and has no odor,

But it is pure as the snow and will clean our minds because the Lord has shown is favor.

I will worship and praise your name,

Because my life has not been the same.

I accept your son in my heart; please never let your Holy Spirit part from my soul

I have faith in you, so I want you to tell me and lead me in the righteous thing to do

I will claim your precious son Jesus

I'm so happy that your spirit came in my heart

I need you in the morning and late at night.

When my flesh gets weak, teach me how to fight, with your holy spirit.

Talk to my spirit because I will need to hear it, way down in my soul.

Because I wish to hold your precious face, help me run this Christian race.

I repent of all my sins, so let your spirit live from within.

My soul is like a sweet melody because you are my savior

I am somebody, special

As I witness your precious grace please don't erase all the mercy you poured on me.

Because your mercy has set us free, what does the Lord require is to do? "Believe"

And receive his precious son Jesus.

I am beautiful

They say that beauty is in the eye of the beholder,

So I believe that I am a beautiful soldier.

That God has created,

I am beautiful! Because God loves me,

Because his beauty has set me free.

I am beautiful!

Because I am Calvary where Jesus Christ has died for me.

I am beautiful!

Because when I was a little girl,

I accepted Jesus into my world!

I am beautiful!

Far as the Nile River in Egypt and the deep blue sea,

From descendants of Kings and Queens in Africa, is where my dark skin originated

Since the beginning of civilization where God was first created.

I am black, a color that refers to power and wealth.

Because god loved us before we loved our self,

So if I don't love myself, then I can't expect (love) from anyone else.

Because I am beautiful!

Deep love

When I say I love you it's for real.

A love that is so deep,

Like the bottom of the ocean, and a tranquil night sleep.

And your heart holds a special place for that person

A love that I always wanted to pursue.

It's like when you stay up all night long,

And you feel that person could do no wrong.

A love that comes from above,

A love that is as gentle as a dove,

A love so deep it has set me free.

Because of your grace you have put a sweet taste in my mouth

And your spirit has touched my soul, and made me whole.

I will stay in the Lord's will until his prophecy is fulfilled.

Bless me O' Lord because I have obeyed and trusted in thy word, have mercy on me, lord.

I am a sinner and I need your help!

Restore my soul and renew a righteous spirit within me,

I offer myself to you lord because of love.

You are the deep love that I have been looking for.

Youths shot and killed

One youth,

Two youth,

Three young youth,

Four youth,

Five youth,

Six youth,

Seven young youth,

Eight youth,

Nine youth,

Ten young youths shot and killed this year!

Stop the violence!

Don't Kill Our Youths!

Lord, When Will It End?!

A broken spirit

Yeah! Satan you tried to make us bow to your silly tricks.

Well! I want you to listen to this. Jesus died and kicked you out of Heaven.

Stop messin' with God children 24/7.

You have no power, so leave this place and never came back,

Because we don't want to see your face.

We are Christians and prepared to fight

God will shine his mercy because you have no light!

Our hearts may be broken, but our spirits will win.

Because Jesus will be victorious if we ask him to forgive us of our sins.

And he will mend us of our broken hearts.

We will proclaim victory and glory in Jesus name, so stop pretending to have fame!

You have no soul; your heart is evil and cold.

Always bragging that you are the best, never passing the test,

Your spirit I just want to forget.

I know that you are an evil foe, who preys on those who just don't know,

because they are weak and have no power.

So it's not even about you, because you are evil works are through.

Get lost! At any and all cost, and if you really want to hear it,

I had a broken spirit.

Then I asked God to open up my heart and come in and forgive me of my sins.

And my spirit the Lord did mend!

Gangs

Young people join gangs because they want to be accepted,

Then once they join, they find out that they have been deceptive.

Don't join gangs because you are better than that.

You have the potential to be a leader and wear many hats.

Some gangs rob, steal and kill, and that is not God's will, for you,

God wants you to use your heart and mind for good.

Just like a loyal solider should.

It's so easy to do bad things,

And the consequence is death, that's all it brings.

Do the right thing and live longer,

And let your character get stronger.

Don't be a thug and sell those drugs.

There's a lot of good inside you that can be found.

What good are you in jail or dead on the ground?

Don't join gangs! Live Life.

A Conscience Effort

One of the golden rules,

Was to make good grades in school

Then you go to college to further your knowledge.

To always try to do what is right,

And never get into a fight.

Always lend a helping hand,

And pick up those who cannot stand.

Be a leader in everything you do,

Instead of giving an old gift, bring something new.

Give from your heart, that's a good start.

Where there is a will, make a way.

Love one another every day,

Keep these conscience efforts in mind,

Then you well be, just fine.

God's Grace

God is so great that he gives us his love.

An unwarranted favor that comes from above.

He has shown his grace in many ways,

By giving us his salvation from day to day.

While on this earth realm we will sin.

But if we ask for forgiveness he will wash away them,

And makes us whole again.

And because we love God of our free mind,

He will bless us all the time.

We all have a cross to bare,

So if we repent the Lord will be there,

By our side to guide us through,

All of the trials and tribulations.

Because it was his blood that was shed for our salvation.

Lord bless this nation and all that call upon your precious name,

Because that is why your Holy Spirit came.

To save those that were last,

You sent your son Jesus that died on the cross.

I was so happy I gave my heart to him, because his grace and mercy has set me free.

When I was blind, now I see that the Lord's love was there for me.

I am a sinner and I need your help.

Teach us how to love you, more than ourselves

Because if we love you, there will be no more strife.

Save us Lord so we have eternal life.

If you play with fire, you will get burned!

If you play with fire, you will get burned.

This is a lesson people should learn.

Experimenting with sex when you're not ready.

Just hold on to Jesus word and you'll be steady, and not confused.

Keep the word of God on your heart and tell someone if you have been abused.

Learn how to get help, quick.

Because that behavior is unacceptable and not always easy to fix.

If you don't get help you'll continue this vicious cycle with your kids or other

people's kids and that's just not the right thing to do, you know.

Because everyone has to one day, reap what they sow.

It's not easy to talk about, but it happens more than you think.

Get some counseling from the Lord, so you won't sink into a false sense of security?

That's why God, sent his son Jesus to die so you will have life, eternity.

Don't let your flesh get the best of you ask God for guidance, he'll see you through.

Because if you play with fire you will get burned!

Read the word of God, walking like Jesus is a lesson we all should do and learn!

Jail is hell!

Always do the right thing, or else you will wind up dead or in jail.

And jail is hell!

In jail they feed bread and water, they have no freedom like a person ought a!

Always looking over your shoulder while the nights gets colder and colder,

This is not living, it is just surviving.

While you see if a visitor will be arriving, some will come for awhile,

Just to see you smile.

And the stories you will tell jail is hell!

Well let me tell you something my child,

You will never go to jail because you gave you heart to Christ.

The love of God will ever fail you,

Because God's love will see us through and teach and guide you to do the right thing, too

since you have given him your life.

You now have grace and eternal life,

So don't do the crime if you can't do the time;

without a doubt Jesus has brought you out of your despair,

now you know his spirit is always there.

His mercy you just can't compare!

Because of love he has unlocked the key,

No longer chained, now you are free!

Lord, show us the way!

If you have been mistreated or physically, emotionally, mentally abused, and you are confused.

Don't blame yourself; get some help from the Lord or tell someone about the abuse.

Ask the Lord for guidance so you will understand that Satan is the author of confusion,

And in Jesus Christ we will stand.

Ask the Lord for forgiveness and pray every day.

Lord, please, just show me the way!

When there is no hope and no one seem to care, call on Jesus,

Because our sins he did bear.

Even if you are a straight up thug,

And you get hooked on those drugs.

And family and friends are not around, don't you give up or give in,

With the Lord, Jesus you can win,

Because once we were lost, now we are found.

Lord, show us the way.

When you have a disease and the doctor have given up on you,

God will see you through.

Just put your trust in him and pray.

Lord show us the way!

If you are alone and wondering if anyone will ever love you,

God will reveal that if you love yourself,

Wait on him to remove that sadness and pain.

And he will give you your heart, body, and soul again.

Just seek his Holy Spirit, because it will make a way, every day.

Lord, show us the way!

Do unto others as you would want them to do to you, don't get love twisted,

Because the Lord is always true, and righteous.

Ask God for this mercy and guidance every day.

And pray the Lord, to show you the way.

I am lost without you!

Sometimes I want the pleasure of this world and my mind wonders,

Then I go outside and I see the rain and hear the thunder!

Then I ask myself, why am I here?

Sometimes I don't want to know the answer, because of fear.

I am lost without you!

If I surrender my all, will I fall and come short by your precious grace.

So I ask for forgiveness, so I will see your precious face.

When this world is no more,

Your holy spirit will endure.

I am lost without you!

As I sit and write these words I don't know if they will ever be heard!

So just in case they are, I know your spirit will be near, not far.

I am lost without you!

If my actions are found to be true and sincere,

You will always be near and a true friend,

So I will not fear.

I am lost without you!

I found your holy spirit within

This special feeling I hope will never end,

Because your goodness and mercy shall follow me through the rest of my life,

No longer lost, I have found that peace that will endure forever.

Thank you lord, because with you I found myself.

Coming into the light

Dark deep despair,

No one seems to care,

Pain too hard to bare,

The road is dim and darkness makes it hard to see.

Hear a good word,

That you never heard,

You were singing the blues,

Now you hear the good news.

The road is clearer, vision is,

Clearer, you see a glimmer,

You change your life,

Bye giving it to Christ.

Now the road seems near,

The vision is now clear,

I can rest at night because I see the light.

I hear the word,

I believe the word,

I saw the word, and the word was Jesus, now I see the light.

If you want to be strong

If you're all alone,

You got to be strong.

If you want to have a friend,

You have to look within.

If you want someone to love you,

You have to love yourself.

When you're in trouble,

You got to get some help!

If you want to be strong, don't try to do it on your own.

I'm here for you, no matter what you do.

If you need someone to comfort you, I'll be around.

Everyone needs somebody, when they go through ups and downs.

I'll be your sweet angel to take you by the hand,

With wisdom there to guide you, I'll do the best I can.

If you need someone to talk to, I'll have an open ear,

To listen to all your troubles, just talk because I am here!

If you want to be strong, I'll be there, just hold on.

Open up your heart and I will never part.

My spirit will be there to make you strong,

So you won't ever be alone.

Just call me, I will set you free!

You opened up your heart, now I will never part.

Lord, you move me!

I call upon the lord and he has set me free

I gave him my soul, now I am free

In him is where one day I will be

As I run this Christian race,

I will pray every day so in my heart you will live and stay!

Lord, you move me!

I will jump up and down

When your spirit comes pouring down.

Lord, you move me!

As I wave my hands form side to side

I will trust in thee, because you sent your son Jesus to die, for me

Lord, you move me!

As I seek your face no one will take your place,

In my heart, because from the start, you loved me.

Lord, you move me!

Oh! Happy days when Jesus washed all our sins away

When we look at the rainbow in the sky,

It should remind us of the day that the Lord washed our sins away.

Just give your life to Jesus then he will come in and wash away all your sins.

One day as I was driving by,

I saw a rainbow in the sky.

There was no pot of gold at the end of this rainbow,

Because it was a reminder when Jesus washed away our sins,

And saved our soul and made us whole again.

That rainbow was so beautiful and it spoke to my heart,

Saying if you believe in my son my love will never depart.

The colors of that rainbow were pink, blue, orange, yellow, red, and purple.

Pink is for love that is God and comes from above,

Blue is for the Heaven and skies that Is God's home.

If we put our faith in God we will never be alone.

Blue is also when God sent his son Jesus and made the ultimate sacrifice.

Because of his grace and mercy, we now have everlasting life.

Orange is for the joy that is all around because when we gave our heart to Christ,

That the passion of love was found.

Yellow is for the bright sun, because as Christians our work is never done.

But if we keep the faith, our Lord's kingdom will come.

Red is the power in the blood that Jesus shed for our sins.

Purple is for royalty, because God is king and Jesus is his prince,

And because of God compassion he sent his son Jesus to die for our sins,

And wash them all away!

Oh! Happy days when Jesus washed all my sins away!

Then I look at the Earth and see the beauty of all things God created,

Like brown for nature, because God so loved the world he gave his only son to die

for our sinful nature.

My God is also the creator, because he created the world, life, and all that is nature, everywhere.

So at the end of this Earth realm I will say: It was a happy day Lord, when you washed my sins away!

Blood on the throne

I am the way, truth, and the life that is what Jesus said,

as they pierced a crown of thorns on his head.

And for that, God cried when they killed his son, Jesus said let thy will be done,

and the lord sent him home.

But there was blood on the throne,

because God sent his son to pay the ultimate price;

so that we would have everlasting life.

Some people still don't believe that he is the Christ, and there was blood on his throne.

Come my children unto me and Jesus said that he will set you free.

So I gave my heart and soul to him, because I once was lost,

but now I'm found and that in heaven with him is where I want to be.

When he calls my name one day to leave this Earth realm and go home, I won't be alone,

because it's his blood on the throne.

The blood that give us strength from day to day and will never lose its power.

Lord bless us with your Holy Spirit; let it rain down on us like a shower,

So we can grow in your word every hour.

Your precious spirit set the tone, because there is blood on the throne.

As Jesus spirit ascended to Heaven and the gates of Hell did not prevail,

when they hung him on the cross his hands and feet they did nail.

He cried out to his father, God, and he was not alone.

There was blood on the throne!

Jesus blood was shed for our sins, when Christ died on the cross.

The Heaven rejoiced when the precious lamb came home,

because there was blood on the throne.

Gun Control

How many bullets does it take to kill a man?

Piercing through his soul again and again

Did you think he was a snob?

So you had to finish the job.

Some people have no respect for life,

Whether it's at the hands of a gun or a knife.

Yet, because you wear a badge, do you think its right?

To end a human life?

Do you think that you are the judge and jury? That's what courts are for

But you are the law, so civil injustice you just ignore.

Take control of your gun; don't let yourself get out of control.

Think of other than yourself!

Because if you lose control, it can mean someone's death.

I am alive because of God's mercy

Jesus died because of our sins God loved the world he gave his only son, to die on the cross.

To save our souls and forgive our sins, when we were lost.

It is his blood that was sacrificed so we may have everlasting life,

So if we accept him in our hearts we are now free!

I am alive because of God's mercy,

Every day I live, is because of God's love.

His spirit is so sweet and it come from up above!

It is your Holy Spirit that taught us how to pray:

Now I lay me down to sleep I pray the Lord my soul to keep,

If I should die before I wake,

I pray the Lord my soul to take all that I ask in Jesus name.

Amen.

Thank the Lord!

Who is the word?

In the beginning I have heard there was Jesus, he was the word.

He was with God in the beginning and we must ask him for forgiveness when we are sinning.

Who is the word?

The word is Jesus, he is the beginning and ending of this life.

So give your life to him and you will be free and see that he is the light of the world.

In him I will trust! Because he is one us! God made him human to live among us,

He made man in his image from the dust.

Who is the word?

The word is the Holy Spirit that will set us free, as he died on Calvary.

In him we should give our hearts and believe.

Who is the word?

Love is God,

Jesus is the word.

The word was with God in the beginning and if we believe,

He will forever live in our hearts.

I'll fight for you!

When everyone else turns their back on you,

I will be there to see you through.

Don't ever think that you are all alone or on your own,

My spirit will be there for you too,

I'll fight for you!

When this world seems so cold,

And your enemies are getting bold,

I'll fight for you!

When your heart is burning and your soul is set on fire,

I'll be there to put out the fire, and quench your earthly desires.

I'll fight for you!

Even when the wind blows and it rains.

I'll be there to ease the pain,

And give your life to sustain.

I'll fight for you!

When you are concerned and there was no way out!

I'll be there to erase all doubts,

And fears. I will wash away your tears.

I'll fight for you!

I will be there, through thick and thin,

Because with your spirit we will win.

In you I have found a confidant and a friend.

I know your love will always be there, even in the end.

Let your kingdom come, because the battle has been won!

Victory is ours.

Over the rainbow, where angels fly,

Your life has just begun.

Love will always triumph,

When we fight for what is right.

When there isn't anything to praise you for, Lord

Bad news came too fast, my spirit is crying out!

Lord! How long will this last, the pain is too hard to bare.

I am so numb and down in the dumps it's hard for me to even care,

Times are so hard; still I call on you Lord.

When there isn't anything to praise you for Lord.

So I am reaching out, please hold my hands and get me out of this sinking sand.

You are the solid rock so let me stand

When there is nothing to praise you for Lord!

I don't know wrong from right; please just show me your holy light.

Because in you I trust keep my mind right and keep our flesh from this lust,

Because the lust of this world is full of desire,

Lead us in your word so we can pour water on this fire that is burning up our souls.

Because it is you, we wish to behold one day teach us to pray.

When there isn't anything to praise you for.

Well I am alive and I have survived all their trials and tribulation.

Because I call your name, my life has never been the same

Praise the lord because he is the rock of my salvation.

Believe, Receive and Achieve

As I was walking the spirit was talking way down in my soul,

Telling me "Believe and receive that I'll set you free!"

Accept that his word is true,

Because it is right thing to do.

Hold his spirit close to your heart,

Because his love was there from the start.

And his word people need to hear!

Greet his spirit as a welcomed friend, and then your soul will have to fear!

Let his love live within, present him with your soul and mind,

Give him all your cares and burdens to lighten up your load.

Offer him your life because his son paid the price.

So that if we believe we'll have everlasting life.

If we believe and receive, his spirit will be there to carry us through all life's trials and tribulations.

Accept and believe his word,

You will always be on speed dial,

To his mercy and grace.

Believe and receive that if we trust him, we will achieve our goals.

His spirit will show us the holy way to go.

Because it is his spirit that one day we will behold,

If we just believe!

Worthy is the Lamb

I will praise you lord every day in every way, because you are worthy to praised!

Worthy is the lamb, let your blessing come down, and the power

Of your Holy Spirit show its glory!

Let us praise you and don't be in a hurry, to let your spirit go.

So we can bathe in the Holy Spirit and your grace and mercy flow.

Worth is the lamb!

Lead us in the path of righteousness so we can do your will.

Because you sent your son Jesus so we can live!

Worthy is the lamb

I hear your voice call my name and I am so glad you came, to show you're a kind, sweet spirit.

Worthy is the lamb

I need you to guide and protect me from all harm.

And keep my heart wrapped in your arms. So I can see you are the light of the world.

You are the great I am, and your precious blood was shed for us to cleanse our souls

Making us whole, we were told of the story about your glory and it has set us free.

Precious Lamb of God you are worthy to be praised and glorified, because you sent

Jesus to bleed and die for our sins, now his spirit lives within my soul,

And its holy presence has taken control of my life.

When the wind blows!

When the wind blows, nobody knows how it feels as it caresses our bodies

And touches our face.

The cool air feels so mesmerizing, tantalizing, hugging us with its embrace.

When we close our eyes, the breeze let us know that we are alive;

So we live another day and thank the Lord that we're O.K.!

The wind calms our souls and makes us want to stay outside,

Where the breeze is blowing leaves on the Trees

As they fall to the ground. Not making a sound.

When the wind blows!

Living things play around as the birds fly high and began to sing their songs.

When the wind blows!

Your love will lift us up higher, far above the ground; your love is all around.

It has set our souls on fire! No longer do we have earthly desires.

Because the love that you have given us has set us free!

Now it is your love that I pray, that will save us each day.

From the temptations of this world, because when we called your name,

Our life never was the same.

We gave you our hearts and your blood flows, whenever we feel the wind blow!

Nobody knows the changes we have gone through,

Because we gave our hearts to you.

When the wind blows!

When we die, that's where we will meet one another in the sky, as angels spreading our wings.

When the wind blows and the angels sing!

Repentance

God's grace and mercy is nothing new, but when we repent we change our attitudes.

It is when we ask him to forgive our sins and turn from our sinful ways.

Because though we were in darkness, now we see the light in you, so we trust you every day.

And by your grace we live so we ask the Lord for our sins to be forgiven

And come onto our hearts.

Because you change our minds and now we have a new start.

Please keep us on track so we will always look forward and never back!

Renew our minds, so we will find another way,

To follow you more nearly and love you more dearly.

Never will I doubt, your love because it is real,

And I won't stop praising you until your precious angel takes me home.

It is your love that will keep us safe and warm at night,

So my soul will know everything will be alright.

I am calling on your Holy Spirit to see me through all the perils of this world,

So when I get to heaven, I will know that because I repented of my sins,

You made me whole and now I know that I am born again and my heart is as pure as snow.

THE POETIC COURIER III

Final Chapter

(True salvation lives within)

These are the final chapters of the poetic courier; I wish to thank my sons Lewis, Isaac, and Vincent Turner; Family and friends

Victory in Jesus!

When the enemy (which is Satan) is near, have no fear, because we are God's children.

When we were lost, now because of Jesus we have been found.

We are proud warriors, fighting in a war and in Jesus we have the victory,

That will set us free of the pain and through him we are healed once again.

Just give him all your worries and fears today! And he will wash them all away.

He'll give you strength day by day, trust in him he will make a way!

So keep praying and saying that it's ok, because God sent his son Jesus to set me free.

And in him I have the victory.

Blessed is the Rock of my Salvation!

Lord, bless this Nation and the whole World of God's creation.

Blessed is the Rock of my Salvation.

Lord, just guide and take my hand,

And give me wisdom to understand

That when all other ground sinking sand you will stand

Tall, like no one else can.

You are the rock of my Salvation.

Blessed is the Rock of my Salvation is a dedication to a solid foundation,

That will never fall, because his Holy Spirit will answer when I call.

When I leave this troubled land I will seek God's helping hand,

And my soul will rejoice when I hear his beautiful voice, saying welcome home my child.

Then the angels shall sing so beautiful and loud in a city far above the clouds,

And there will be no temptation.

Blessed is the Rock of my Salvation.

I will praise you all the time because your spirit is worthy and divine, praise be to our lord.

Because you love us so much I see, that's why you sent your son Jesus to die for me.

Because it was Jesus that held the key to unlock my soul and now I'm free.

Blessed is the Rock of my Salvation!

Who is God?

God is Love.

A spirit that is sweet, yet so simple and comes from above.

My son said that there is no God,

So that means he has the mind of an atheist.

I was horrified and puzzled by this thought.

How could he make such a statement!

How could he believe that God does not exist,

When he created him and gave him life.

Because of that love, if he believe than,

He too will have everlasting life.

How could he not believe that God sent his son Jesus to die for our sins?

When he made the ultimate sacrifice, his love now lives within.

If I ever had to sacrifice my son for the sins of the world,

I don't think that I would, for God so loved this sinful world that he really could, and did.

That is why I would defend the Lord at any cost,

because that is why his only son died to save those that were lost.

As I pondered and wondered where these thoughts were coming from,

My son's father died when he was very young.

This may be why my son is so angry, but blaming God is just not right.

How could he not believe that God's son Jesus died for his life?

And if we believe in him, will have eternal life,

And if we ask, then he will come in, our hearts and take us by the hand.

He failed to understand, why his father was not there,

When he became a man.

His father gave his life to Christ, and because of that he has eternal life.

Well, let me tell you something my child,

God picked you out of the crowd.

Because your life is important, I experience the true joy that as a mother,

This life could bring,

So when you were born I heard the angels of the Lord sing.

You are a part of our Heavenly Father's unconditional love that was there from the start,

Because of that your earthly Father and Father in Heaven will always love you,

And their love will always be in a special place in your heart.

Heart and soul

My soul pumps the blood to my veins,

Like when Jesus died and we are born again.

The heart pumps blood throughout the body so we can live,

When God gave his son Jesus, he gave all he could give.

That's how much he loved us and because of that in him I trust.

I give you my heart and my soul.

So when I die, it is you I will behold,

My heart and soul will go to a higher place.

When my spirit is blessed by your grace,

I will praise you all the time because you are all mine,

And I am grateful you love me enough to give your life,

So I might have life everlasting and the peace and joy it brings.

I will do your will and won't give up until,

You call me home, someday and lord I will pray every day that you'll stay,

In my heart and soul so I can live, forever.

If

If I was life, I would give my heart to Christ. I would have the power to heal, and there would

Never be any disease and Heaven would be on Earth.

Everyone would receive a rebirth and no one will be ill.

If:

I was a king I would give my life to Christ, because he is worthy of praise and he would be king.

If:

I was holy I would lift my hands up to God and worship him in his sanctuary.

If:

I was God, I would be love.

If:

I was a dancer; I would dance for the lord, because we have the victory that will set us free.

If:

I was a sinner, I would ask for forgiveness, because if we ask we shall receive.

If:

I was mercy; I'd be fixed when I am broken. Have mercy on me Jesus.

If:

I was a servant; I would serve the lord every day of my life.

If:

I was faith, I would believe that his word is the truth and he will set me free.

If:

I believe in you lord, I am free.

If:

I was death you have no sting, because I will walk with Jesus in heaven, and that would be A beautiful thing.

Depression

Never let life get you down. Trust in the lord, he will always be around.

When things are not going your way, that's the time that you should pray.

And ask God for guidance and grace. So we can run and finish this Christian race.

Don't sleep all the time, get out of that bed!

Don't you know you are a walking angel that Jesus, blood was shed, for.

Don't give up! Trust in him and you will endure all of life's trials and tribulations.

Believe in the lord, for a glorious celebration.

Be happy because you are free and are alive to worship the lord.

So praise him with one accord and kick the depressed spirit to the curb.

Because your prayers have been heard. No longer bound,

The secret of true happiness is the love of the God you found.

So behold, don't lose your soul!

What good is it if you obtain all the riches of the world and lose your soul?

That is just too much of a sacrifice to give away. Give your heart and soul to God today.

He'll be there to hold your hand and also be a friend.

So behold, don't lose your soul! When this life gets you down,

My sweet savior will always be around.

Believe in him and he will make a way.

So behold, don't lose your soul!

Behold his glory presence found listen to his voice, what a beautiful sound.

It's so easy to give your heart to him,

all you have to do is believe, and he will set you free.

So behold, don't lose your soul!

Accept him in your heart today and continue to read and hear his word

And pray every day!

Suicide- The easy way out!

There is no honor in suicide; it's the easy way out!

Just give your troubles and cares to Jesus,

He will erase all of our doubts and fears.

And when we are crying, he'll wash away our tears.

Just because you're a good person doesn't mean you'll go to heaven,

Have faith above all things.

Giving up means that person has failed to see the beauty and joy that life brings.

The opposite of that beauty is misery and pain.

Give your life to the lord and he will ease that pain.

Seek the lord, and his wisdom then you will be whole again.

Trust in the lord, he'll bring you out of any situation, just hold onto his sweet hands,

And he'll guide you through all trials and tribulations.

Hold on to his love that comes from above, and he won't let you down.

He will always be around, to carry you through life's ups and downs, every day.

Live life every day, suicide is not the way.

A person can lose fame, money, cars, etc. Don't lose your soul.

As Christians we must be bold warriors ready to fight.

Killing yourself is just not right.

Ask for help! That's not a sign of weakness, but strength.

Stay alive at any length.

And when we have prayed and God is ready to take us home,

We will never be depressed, sad, or alone.

Suicide is never the answer we have a choice,

Choose life and above all, "Love yourself".

Forgiveness

One day in praise an inmate gave his heart and soul to Christ.

This inmate was in prison for murder so he will be there locked up

for the rest of his life.

He killed his wife, so now his kids don't have a father or mother.

Now Child Protective Services gave his kids to the closest relative, his brother.

Growing up without a mother was really tough, but his kids were there when

Their mom died so they witnessed first-hand the disturbing sight.

How could they ever forgive him, for ruining their life, by killing their mother, and his wife?

This was all too hard to bear, and at first he just didn't seem to care.

Then years passed and one day that prisoner gave his heart to Christ, and accepted our Lord,

First he asked for forgiveness from the Lord, then from his children.

So his children forgave him and let the anger go.

Because they also accepted the Lord and his spirit opened their hearts to forgive,

Now that prisoner has been set free even though he is still in jail, because he asked God

for forgiveness he won't go to hell!

With the Lord we will win if we ask him to forgive our sins because his grace and mercy,

will see us through.

When we ask him for forgiveness, he will always be there to show us the right thing to do.

Restore my soul lord!

Dear lord, hear my prayers.

Restore my soul so that I will praise and worship you.

Like a good Christian should do.

I am a lowly Shepard seeking your will for my life.

Every day the wolves come after my soul, teach me how to fight.

Restore my soul lord!

When I am sick on my death bed and I need a friend in you II will depend.

You are the only one that can help me now!

I know that your spirit will heal my body somehow!

You have the power to give life and death.

Restore my soul lord!

When there is nothing left to fight for.

Everyone has to die one day.

Restore my soul lord!

So I can live another day, to praise and worship you.

Love is not dead!

God is love, and he is not dead! I promised to love and cherish you for the rest of my life,

Till death do us part. Death came early, but you will remain forever in my heart.

Love is not dead!

Trying to go on with my life was a hard thing to do.

But love goes on, even without you!

Love is not dead!

I ask for mercy but god gave forgiveness instead. And I thank the lord for that,

Because that is why his son Jesus blood was shed.

Love is not dead!

Because he loved us unconditionally, his love will set us free, free of all worries and fears,

That is what I want to hear! Because we all have our own cross to bear.

Love is not dead!

Thank you for being around, when I was down. Without a doubt with your love I was found.

By your grace and mercy, I have been set free, and now I see, it is your love, and with you

Is where I want to someday be.

It's a great feeling to know his love for us will grow. Because when we seek his face for guidance

He will show us the way to go, and also because the Bible tells us so!

Love is not dead!

God rose on the third day from the dead, by his spirit we will be led.

And because God is love, I am glad that he's spirit is alive in my heart and will never depart.

Instead I am happy, not sad. Because God is love and he's not dead!

Love is not dead!

Today's Pharisees (holier-than-thou)

In ancient times, I have been told,

There were priest that would heal your souls.

But that was long ago, when Jesus came upon this land.

He was there to guide and take his people's hand.

He healed the sick and hung out with the poor.

A forgotten people that the Pharisees ignored.

Back then church folks just did not understand.

How a man name Jesus could heal people with the touch of his hand.

How he made the crippled walk and the blind to see,

And how he delivered lepers from demons and set the people free.

Who is this man? They say he was a demon, just because he made miracles

and preached the good news of the kingdom.

He gave his 12 disciples authority to drive out demons and unclean spirits,

And heal every kind of disease.

But when the Pharisees heard about these miracles and wonders,

They did not know what to do as they began to ponder.

What should we do about this man who says that he is a God and not a man?

Jesus was only doing his father God's will, and for that he was hung and killed.

Now, anyone that is lost can take up his cross and follow him.

But those Pharisees could never hear the Lord's voice or understand his Holy Spirit,

Even though they saw all the miracles that were done,

They could not comprehend how God loved the world so much that he sacrificed his only son.

Church people let's lead our people in the righteous way,

And love one another every day.

Let us become fisherman, so we can catch fish.

Because when the blind lead, the blind, they will both fall in the ditch.

Let us pray every day that the Lord, Jesus, will show us the way,

Then we will not be like the Pharisees to holier- than- thou to bow to our Lord every day!

When the rain came down!

If you look close with your eyes and listen,

Then you will hear the rumbling sound of thunder and smell the rain as it gets closer,

Then minutes later the rain will come down.

There will be pelting sounds as the wind blows as the grass moves back and forth.

The trees sway from side to side, while the birds take cover and hide

From the pelting stings, when down comes the rain.

It's crackling sound all around as it hits my window pane, again and again.

First there are little sprinkles,

Then those drops get turned into showers and never stop!

Falling and creatures on this Earth, as it begins to sing.

When the rain comes down!

We will hear different sounds in the air,

Like the rumbling of thunder and lightning that is so frightening.

When the rain comes down!

We know that the earth will grow, because it is nature's way of letting us know

That the Lord lives!

Pour your Holy Spirit down on us!

When we hear the thunder the rain will come to make the plants grow,

This you can trust!

Pour your Holy Spirit down on us!

So like the plants so we can grow in your spirit and became soldiers in your army.

Let us praise you with a song all night long.

Let us praise you with a dance.

Let your body go and give God a chance.

Let's clap, snap, and rap to God's heartbeat,

So we can move our feet and give him the praise.

Pour your Holt Spirit down on us!

If your God's child just raise your hand from side to side,

And sing and shout to the power of the lord comes through.

Pour your Holy Spirit down on us!

We will dance, shout, and magnify your name,

We are so glad you came, and poured your spirit down on us!

Hollywood Blues!

What's the difference between the ghetto and Hollywood?

There's not much. Hollywood is supposed to be glamorous. Light camera, action.

Beautiful homes and attractions, on the other hand, they are similar.

In the ghetto there's a lot of drugs around and in Hollywood, there is also a lot of drugs.

The only difference is that in the ghetto it will get you behind bars.

Hollywood drugs are a culture and you mingle with the stars.

In the ghetto, when a person gets hooked on drugs, they're considered a crack head!

People get on drugs in Hollywood, they are addicts, it has been said.

In the ghetto they light up the sky with bullets.

In Hollywood they glorify killing and are full of it.

There certain aspects in the ghetto like prostitutes, pimps, drive by shootings, killing in joints,

You get the point.

In Hollywood there's red carpets symbolizing glamour and wealth.

Everyone in Hollywood interact among themselves, allegedly.

Whether you live in Hollywood or the ghetto, one thing remains the same,

We all must call upon the lord, Jesus, to be saved and reborn again.

Rich keep getting rich I'm just getting "po"

When I look at the world, I feel it's not fair that some people just don't want to share

They want the whole world in their hand, and sometimes I just can't understand why

They don't want to give. Say it ain't so.

> Rich keep getting rich,
>
> I'm just getting "po"

Then I think to myself, is it really fair that we should ignore those people who are in despair

And the congress really doesn't care, about the poor. Are they friend or foe?

> Rich keep getting rich,
>
> I'm just getting "po"

Why should the government subsidize your constitution and give the banks all that cash.

There not even giving loans, their just keeping their stash, telling consumes (borrowers)

To dash for the door and don't come back no more.

    Rich keep getting rich

    I'm just getting "po"

Don't get mad cause it's too bad that you just don't want to know.

    Rich just keep getting rich

    I'm just getting "po"

Hosana! Blessed be the rock

Lord, you are worthy to be praised, with our hands; we will clap and raise them up high!

And worship your sweet spirit, every day until we see your glory in the sky.

We will praise you in the morning noon, and night,

So let your spirit shine its light!

Hosana! Blessed be the rock.

Jesus is the rock that we stand,

All other ground is sinking sand.

When we are in trouble, if we ask for help,

His spirit will guide us with his holy hands.

Hosana! Blessed be the rock.

I will say yes, to your will so your prophecy will be fulfilled

And you Holy Spirit we will feel.

Lord, don't let this feeling ever end!

Hosana! Blessed be the rock.

In you I will trust, because you are creator.

Bless my soul and this nation.

Hosana! Blessed be the rock of my salvation.

I need your love all the time because my heart and soul will accept your loving grace.

At the end of thy realm on this Earth I want to see your precious face.

Bless my spirit Jesus because your love is heavenly divine.

It is with you I want to be at the end of time.

Your love has set us free because of that I dedicated my life to you.

I know it's you that will see me through!

Hosana! Blessed Jesus you are the rock of my salvation!

Heavenly Dove

Heavenly Dove was sent from above.

Take flight and spread your wings as you fly through the sky.

Teach us how to love and do that is right,

Show us your glory & shine your light,

Bless our souls, when you take flight.

Touch our heart and never depart your spirit, wisdom and grace,

Teach us how to run this Christian race.

Stay and comfort us in our time of need

When our path is dark and we are afraid,

Lead us in the righteous path every day.

With your wings hold our hearts,

And never take your love away or depart.

An impossible mission

I can do all things with Christ that strengthens me!

He's the only one that can set you free.

Free from all worries and stress give it all, to the lord, Jesus and he will do the rest.

It is fear that is the author of confusion.

Satan handy craft works of delusions. But Jesus died, so we can live in harmony.

We have to trust him to give us the victory and triumph over the enemy.

An impossible mission you say!

Not impossible, it's possible today!

Because we are God's children and he has given us power

And as a believer we will win this battle and go home, victorious. Every hour.

When my health fails, Jesus will be there!

When my blood sugar levels are too low or too high and my heart won't pump,

And if I check my breast and find a lump.

> Jesus will be there!

He will be there to see you through, working out a miracle or two.

Trust in him, he'll make a way when your health fails and your body just won't work,

He will heal your aches and pains that hurt!

> Jesus will be there!

When your heart fails and the blood is clogged, he will unclog those arteries and the blood will

Flow through.

> Jesus will be there!

When you check your breast and find a lump,

Don't be in the dump. Just pray and believe that god will heal you.

So when they take that biopsy the mass is not terminal.

> Jesus will be there!

We woke up! Because of God's grace

The Lord woke us up this morning one started us on our way!

He is a mighty God; please help us run this Christian race.

We woke up, Because of God's grace.

The Lord is the beginning and end, and a true friend, if we ask he will forgive our sins.

Every day we live, I want to see k his face,

Because we woke up, because of god's grace.

Your grace is why we live so I ask God for my sins,

Please forgive; it is your goodness that will lead us in the right path.

Because we are obedient children, please spare us from your wrath.

We woke up, because of your grace!

It is because of your grace that we have salvation,

Because your mercy was given reconciliation,

between God and creation.

Lord please bless this nation, so that they will see that it is your grace

and mercy that freed them and ascended them to Heaven.

Because when we wake up in Heaven it is because of your grace.

My Great Redeemer

My Great Redeemer I praise you,

Because you are worthy to praised.

So let us praise your Holy name with our hands raised,

And say yes to his spirit and give him our hearts,

So he will never depart.

My soul will praise and worship your name,

Because you died for my sins that is why you came.

My Great Redeemer.

I open my heart to you, just please,

Help me through all my trials and tribulation,

Restore this soul and bless this nation.

So that they will know that you are what they need,

Teach me to succeed and do your will, and always be present in my soul,

For it's your face I want to behold, someday.

My great Redeemer.

The power of love

The power of love comes from above and is all around,

It's very rare and delicate, like a melody or a beautiful sound.

A sound that echoes all around the world, pulling your heart strings,

The Power of Love can be expressed in words, and songs we sing.

The power of love can be found in many things,

The power of love can be kind, gentle, or meek.

A power that is so strong it can make a person weak,

It's like a baby coming into this world,

Or as simple as a boy meeting a girl.

Then as they mature, that person is still around.

A special bond grown out of that relationship can be found.

Then as time goes by, sharing your love and life,

These two people become man and wife.

Never knowing that their love will stand,

As they hold one another's hand.

Their hearts came together as one, as they cherish and adore one another,

Who knew it would be so grand!

And as they kiss and hug, sharing one another's mug,

The power of love is here to stay,

And we might stay;

"I Love You!", for no reason.

This power of love comes up from above, and will last throughout all seasons.

True Father, Real Man!

God sent his son Jesus down on this Earth as a man.

To guide and teach, so his children will understand how to love and be reborn!

So please Heavenly father, take us by the hand,

Preach your words in our hearts so we will understand and will stand for all that is right.

Let us see your glory and shine down your light!

Teach us how to pray and with you Holy Spirit guide us in the right path,

And let your spirit grow like a flower and shower us with your love every day.

If we are disobedient, chastise us with your mercy and grace,

And be there beside us as we run this Christian race.

Lead us in a righteous way and a straight path,

Because it is your Holy Spirit that when we are obedient and do your will,

That we will receive what we ask.

So lead us to do our best, so we can pass your test.

You are our true father and real man!

So what is a real man you say? He gives his children what is needed every day, a man that will love and cherish his wife.

Like when God sent his son Jesus to make the ultimate sacrifice,

Even though he is just a man, that his wife she will always understand and will take him by the hand,

And do the best she can for him.

True father and real man will go through life's ups and downs,

He will be there for his family when no one else is around.

And will support and guide them through the good and bad times,

because just as God loves his children his love will stand the test of time.

True father, real man!

Will catch his children when they fall down,

And teach them how to stand tall and pray for them when they do wrong,

And let them know that they're not alone.

When they sin, he will let them know that if they ask for forgiveness that AGAPE love

Always will win, and forgive them of their sin.

Will let his family know that his love for them will grow as they receive him in their heart.

And as we take our father by the hand, he will receive us,

Because these are all the qualities we find in our Lord Jesus.

Stand up and give your heart to Christ

If you are in a wheel-chair and cannot get around,

Our Lord's love is a refuge, so it cannot be bound.

You can give your spirit to the Lord, because it is your

Heart and soul where his love is found.

Even if you cannot talk, the Lord will hear you spirit, and it will see you through.

Because it is the Lord's voice that will be heard in our hearts and minds.

Because when were lost, now we are found; was blind, but now can see,

That if we give our heart and soul to the Lord Jesus,

His spirit is with us all the time and will set us free.

Stand up and give your heart and soul to Christ.

Always put the Lord first, and his blessing will follow.

Because what we reap is what we sow!

So never let this world or temptations make you bow,

Because Satan is a defeated foe.

That's why the Lord sent his son Jesus to die for our sins.

It is his Holy Spirit we will win.

So let those old sinful ways go, so he can come in and you will be reborn.

Stand up and give your heart to Christ,

Put his spirit first in your life!

Because it was him that paid the price.

Lord, teach us to strive for the best and always do what is right.

Stand up and give your heart to Christ,

Because the Lord made the ultimate sacrifice when Jesus died on the cross,

Now we can stand tall, because with his grace and mercy we will not fall.

Without a doubt, the lord will be there, when we feel there is no way out.

Stand up and give your heart to Christ,

The Lord is my father and Jesus lives within my heart,

He will forgive all our sins, because his agape love gave us a new start and heart.

Praise the Lord and all that is righteous,

Stand up for the Lord and give your heart to Christ.

When love hurts!

My husband said he didn't want me anymore!

Then just walked right out and closed the door.

When love hurts, the Lord won't desert you!

He will be there to see you through.

My wife and I had a good marriage,

and we got news that we were going have a baby;

Two months later she had a miscarriage.

When love hurts, the Lord won't desert you!

He will be there to see you through!

The doctor told us our child was dying,

When we heard the news we both started crying.

When love hurts, the Lord won't desert you!

He will be there to see you through!

A friend told me he got robbed,

That same day he lost his job.

When love hurts, the Lord won't desert you.

He will be there to see you through!

The hurricane hit and destroyed my house;

killed the kids and spouse.

When love hurts, the Lord won't desert you.

He will be there to see you through!

My child was injured crossing the street,

Now his future is looking bleak.

When love hurts, the Lord won't desert you.

He will be there to see you through!

I came home the other night, my wife and I got into a fight;

When the police came, I'm the one that they blamed.

When love hurts, the Lord won't desert you.

He will be there to see you through!

When my child ran away, and then said he felt all alone;

I told him I did not want him to come back home.

When love hurts, the Lord won't desert you,

he will be there to see you through.

Eat, pray, and exercise is the key

Exercise is the key for our minds and bodies to work properly.

Your body is God's holy temple,

So eat a balanced diet and exercise to keep your body strong;

It's so simple.

Eat right so you will see the light,

Carrots are a vegetable that will make your vision and sight alright!

Exercising in the morning is the best thing to start your day off right,

And help calm the mind. Start with walking, then slight jogs.

Be careful of those neighborhood dogs.

Do modified sit-ups and crunches for that flabby tummy;

So you can be a fantastic looking mommy.

Then go to bed and get 8-10 hours of sleep,

and pray to the Lord for your soul to keep.

"If you should die before you wake, then pray the Lord for your soul to take."

Give your mind, body, and soul to Christ so you can lead a simple life.

Don't party and drink in excess, get up for church on Saturday or Sunday,

And let God handle the rest.

If you follow these simple steps, you will stay away from the Lord's wraith.

Jesus died for bad people too!

Do you think Jesus died because you are a good person?

Think again, he also died for those who are lost.

What do you mean that God died for those that are lost, because all of us have sinned;

But when we ask him to forgive us, he will erase all our sins.

Like it never happened and we are free to love ourselves again,

Because once we were lost, now we have been found through his blood and grace.

Jesus died for the good and bad,

those who are happy and sad.

Those that are black, white, red, and brown; his love for us will never waver.

Because we accepted him, now we are found, and his grace and mercy has shown us favor.

Hear the word at the beginning of time; his spirit is sweet and heavenly divine;

Don't you ever feel sad and blue, because Jesus died for bad people too!

So put God first in your life, do what is right, and don't give up the fight!

Give your heart to him, and let him see you through;

And ask for forgiveness, because Jesus died for bad people too!

Dreams

One day, after my husband died, I thought I saw him, but then realized it was just a dream.

I dreamt he was alive, because I missed him so much;

the way he made me feel and his gentle touch.

Losing a loved one is an experience that is painful, but that pain will help us grow;

And thinking he was alive made me feel like I was sinking to an all-time low.

It was all a dream though in reality my mind was playing tricks on me,

a fragment of my imagination, Even though it seemed so real!

Death of a spouse can make a person depressed, so they don't know how to feel!

Even though I knew my husband was not physically present at night,

His spirit was there to let me know that he was alright.

I know now that I will never see him again on this Earth, so in my mind I celebrate his birth;

Even though it hurts!

Time goes on and I must survive, so it is time to say goodbye, and follow life.

I will have no fear, even though sometimes I feel blue.

In real life my husband was a fairy tale that made all my dreams come true.

Lord you are the air I breathe

We all need water to live and survive, to replenish our body.

Children need to be disciplined when they are naughty,

At the end of time you will pour out your spirit upon all flesh.

Lord, you are the air we need to breathe

I will worship you lord daily, your words

Are food for my soul, and at the end of life,

I want to behold the glory of your spirit.

As I inhale my heart pumps your blood that has set me free,

And I'll never forget all the great things you have done for me,

Lord you are the air I breathe!

When you show me your love through your grace

It's food for my soul and has pleasant taste.

Some don't understand how your mercy works,

Whatever you have done wrong on this Earth, Ask him to forgive you

And it will be done.

Lord, you are the air I breathe!

I will see you when I am broken, there's no doubt

Because I know that the Lord Jesus, will bring me

out of my despair, he will be there.

Lord, you are the air that I breathe.

I will offer myself to him, because he is what I need,

his mercy and grace shall set me free.

It's his blood that was shed, so hear my plea!

Lord, you are the air that I breathe!

Please don't let it be too late to give my heart to you,

To create a new being when the realm of this world is through,

Until then Lord you are the air that I breathe.

A cloud of mercy

As I looked toward the sky and the heavens, I know the Lord is watching over us 24/7.

I feel the wind blowing and its breeze is so easy;

I give praise to the Lord for his son Jesus who has set us free.

The trees seem so happy swaying back and forth,

Because the Lord has supplied all their needs, he is their living source.

Then as I looked in the sky, I saw a cloud floating all alone,

And it revealed to me a spirit whose name was mercy, and it was trying to find its way back home.

That cloud was radiating with compassion which symbolized God's love will be upheld forever,

And even when we suffer the Lord shares our burden.

Together his spirit will see us through the storms of life and protect us in bad weather.

This cloud will be there to stay and never roll away.

Mercy will be there as sure as the sun comes out;

it will embrace us with its love and there will be no doubt,

That cloud of grace will pour down and give us the victory,

Because as a Christian our work is never done, until God's kingdom come.

Because that cloud believed and it trusted in God's word, once lost has been found,

And now glad to be back home safe.

When mercy asked for forgiveness it found its way home it believed and had faith.

When mercy asked for forgiveness, the cloud that was lost has now been found;

Glad to be back home safe from believing and faith.

You will be always in my heart

A letter to my sister

One of the last conversations I had with you was when you said you wanted to go skydiving and I said it wouldn't be a safe thing to do, we both started laughing.

Being the adventurous spirit that you are, I know that you are sky diving in heaven and the clouds have picked up your spirit,

and you are now Free.

Sincerely, Your Sister Genetta

Poetic Courier 1, 2 and 3

Here are some scriptures that I think will be a blessing to you.

Who is God?

Genesis 1:27

John 4:16

Exodus 3:14

Psalms 85:5

Depression

Psalm 34:17

Psalm 40:1 – 3

1 Peter 5: 6 – 7

Romans 8: 38 – 39

1 Peter 4; 12 -13

Suicide

Judges 16: 26 – 30

Revelation 9:6

Genesis 2:7

Forgiveness

Mathew 6: 14 – 15

2 Corinthians 5: 7

Ephesians 1: 7

Daniels 9: 9

Micah 7: 18 – 19

Mathew 6: 9 – 15

Prayers

Mathew 26: 28

Love

John 3: 16

Romans 5: 8

Romans 8: 37 – 38

1 John 3: 1

Romans 13: 8

Ephesians 4: 2

1 John 4: 7

Mathew 6: 23 – 25

John 9 – 17

Scriptures for Grieving

2 Corinthians 1: 3 – 4

Isaiah 41: 10

Psalm 18: 28

Psalm 46: 1 – 2

Revelations 21: 4

Scriptures for Mercy

Mathew 9 – 13

Jude 1: 22 – 23

2nd Chronicles 30: 9

Psalm 86: 5

Revelation 22: 17

Psalm 23: 4

Ecclesiastes 3: 4

2 Samuel 24: 14

Psalm 145: 9

Ephesian 2: 4

Titus 3: 5

Hebrew 4: 16

1 Peter 1: 3

Grace 1 Corinthian 15: 10

Revelation 22: 21

1 Thessalonians 2: 16

1 Timothy 2: 17

2 Corinthians 8: 9

Romans 5: 15

Ephesian 11: 67

Titus 2: 11

2 John 7: 37

Salvation

Psalm 78: 35

Genesis 49: 24

Psalm 18: 31

1 Samuel 2: 2

Deuteronomy 32: 37

Deuteronomy 32: 4

Psalm 92: 15

1 Peter 2: 6 – 7

Psalm 27: 1

Psalm 18: 46

Psalm 62: 7

Psalm 31: 1 – 3

2 Samuel 22: 3